Their Mountain Mother

Their Mountain Mother

The Winter March
Shaka
The Cannibals

Edmund Prestwich

Illustrations Emily Johns

✦ *Edmund Prestwich*

HEARING EYE

Published by Hearing Eye 2009

Hearing Eye
Box 1, 99 Torriano Avenue, London NW5 2RX, UK

ISBN 978-1-905082-46-9

The Cannibals (under the title *Moshoeshoe and the Cannibals*)
and *Shaka* (as *Reign of Blood*) were previously published in *Orbis* magazine.

Designed by Emily Johns
Set in Book Antiqua
Printed and bound by Cambridge University Press

The Winter March

I

My hero is Basutoland's Moshoeshoe —

in the desolate years when wandering hordes,
driven by war and famine, ever fleeing,
spread devastation through the Sotho valleys,
he gathered starving refugees
and made them a new people.

                                            He was born
son of the sub-chief of a tiny clan
in a world of quiet villages where small huts clustered
under enormous mountains, where a boy
would follow the footpaths worn by generations.
He and his age-mates herded his father's sheep;
caught fish and splashed in the river, hunted birds and lizards,
ran races, wrestled, sang, and laughed at women bending
to weed the pumpkin patches. Wars
were cattle raids between adjacent clans,
the death at worst of a fighting man or two;
hunger was the failure of the rains.

At thirty-three he founded his first kraal —
four huts of woven grass and a cattlefold
in a tiny village of his followers

on lands of his First Wife's father. For two years
he watched his handful of young families,
hardworking, full of energy and hope,
building new lives on their patch of hill.
All day his people chanted at their labours.
At night they'd gather in the moonlight, men and women
moving to slow drums, a dance
all rhythmic undulations, whispering
of dry grass wreaths around their wrists and ankles,
the pebbles kissing in small leather pouches;
or men would sit and drink in the council hut.

He shared their joy but he alone was worried.
Rare travellers who walked across the mountains
brought fearful stories from the Nguni clans —
new kinds of war, strange as the wildest legends;
armies that moved in perfect time like dancers,
that ran and fought in thousands, more
than anyone could count, stood face to face
and hacked each other down with stabbing spears;
rivers of blood by hillsides black with corpses;
kraals and villages ablaze, whole clans decamping —
the young men heard it all with childlike wonder,
then laughed and turned away, but not Moshoeshoe.
Could such an army cross the mountains?

A group of friends preparing a stiff leopard skin
will squat in the sun for hours with pots of beer;
they laugh and chatter over it, while all the time,
twisting, kneading, stretching it, stroking it with care,
their fingers work it to the suppleness
that folds you in voluptuously, as warm and soft,

when freezing winds flow down from the Maloti,
as a loving wife when she melts with pleasure.

Just so, Moshoeshoe felt, in his people's way,
a danger to the village should be pondered
by all its men together, taking time
to see it clear and, under the headman's guidance,
to find the right actions and agree on them.
But no-one else could see this danger.
Only with his First Wife, 'MaMohato,
could he speak his thoughts aloud, the firelight sliding
over their naked arms on the lionskin rug,
small points of fire in their anxious eyes.
Sometimes when she turned away to sleep
he'd lie awake. Seeing stars appear
in the smoke-hole as the fire died
he'd think of their lives as refugees —
cut off from crops and cows on the naked mountains,
how could they live like men? Sleeping in caves,
they'd grub for roots with spearblades, frightened always,
like hares or meerkats, staring round them
for hunters to come groping through the rocks.
He pictured Botha-Bothe, the mesa hill
they'd flee up first with its sloping passes.
A narrow neck joined it to the mountains.
It had some grazing land and a good strong spring.
If they could hold that hill and have supplies…
With 'MaMohato's help he forged a plan.

After the harvest and its celebrations,
after the feast, the stories and the singing,

8

he stood before them and began:
"You all have heard of the wise Mohlomi;
I went to visit him before he died. He warned me
of clouds of red dust coming from the east
and mighty armies. I know you all have heard
rumours of great wars among the Nguni.
Perhaps you've been alarmed by them, as I have.
But in these times of need our ancestors
are careful of their children and since then
my great-grandfather has come many times
to speak to me in dreams and give advice."
And so he told them all what they should do.

❂

Months passed. Perhaps there was some muttering.
Then the storm broke and the Wild Cat People came —
a homeless tribe, a ravening human flood,
stripping fields like locusts, fleeing themselves
the amaHlubi from beyond the mountains.
At every kraal they passed they killed and burned,
looted crops and cattle — never enough
to feed the whole horde and let it settle.
Warriors marched in the vanguard: smeared with soot,
mantled in black panther skins, crested with black feathers,
they carried clubs and javelins. Their king's widow,
fierce 'MaNtatisi, strode like a man among them
driving them forward with her violent will.

❂

Two herdboys stand on a grassy hill:
near-naked youths, graceful as tired dancers,
they lean on sticks among their father's sheep.
An afternoon of brilliant heat is cooling.
Shadows of the grass-blades lengthen slowly.

Polished by light, their ebony bodies shining,
they stroll to a cliff edge and stand looking over.

All round them, little sandstone cliffs are glowing,
yellow, molten orange, red, with pools of shadow,
as if the substance of the hills were burning.

A day like any day; till their eyes are caught
by vultures sailing in the air, great lammergeiers
converging in the distance - why so many?
Below the birds there's movement, and a flashing.
A flood of darkness trickles down a valley —
not darkness, living things, that spark with light —
a multitude beyond belief, as if
the stones and grass stems could take human form.

Dropping their sticks, abandoning their sheep
they tumble down the little cliffs,
leaping loose boulders, staggering, lungs on fire,
to shout their warnings to the villagers.
They're hurried to Moshoeshoe, sitting
on the grass by the First Wife's hut, carefully sewing
a soft kaross of otter skins for the winter.
Villagers squat before him waiting to hear
his orders for the harvest. 'MaMohato
stands ready with a pot to pour them beer.

When the clamorous group appears, Moshoeshoe
sees in an instant what they've come to say.
Putting the otter skins quietly aside
he rises to his feet. Decisive, calm,
stilling the leaping fear of his own heart,
he speaks with measured gestures, pitching his voice
above, but just above, the excited cries.
"Now," he says, "we can thank our ancestors
who told us what would come and made us ready.
Now is the time for orderly, quick retreat.
Runners must go everywhere, no herd
or child be left unwarned. Mopeli,
find out who's where and organize the runners.
Someone must hurry to my father's village.
Fetch the last grain from your houses, bring beasts you can catch quickly."
Already as the runners start, perhaps,
they see the first black specks of the horde
breaking a distant ridge. Before it sweeps
into Qhobosheane, screeching battlecries,
waving clubs and javelins, drumming shields,
Moshoeshoe and his people will be gone —
only a white-faced goat will stand in the path
and grain not harvested in the ripening fields.

II

Two years on. The bitterness of winter.
Moshoeshoe's warriors, joined now by his father's,
had watched in despair as horde on starving horde
crowded the valley with their hopeless fires.
How many great and little hordes had passed
while they clung to their mountain, rolling boulders down,
beating off skirmishers, clutching their dwindling grain,
their skinny cows, the frightened, listless wives
and swollen-bellied children in their huts?
Although Moshoeshoe's father, Mokhachane,
was held by all as the whole clan's chief,
only Moshoeshoe and his iron will
had welded them together through that time.
Now with the Wild Cats near again, and seeing
his people weakening almost by the day
he knew they must move on or die.
He sent his brother with a scouting party
to find a safer refuge. When Mohale
returned with news of the perfect hill
and told the clan assembly how it was —
well-watered, broad, precipitous, cut off
on all sides, utterly impregnable,
and hidden from the main path of the hordes —
the warriors' hearts lit up as if they saw it;
but the journey could destroy the clan —
seventy miles, through country swarming
with bands of cannibals and beasts of prey,
the streams mere winter trickles, no villages
to offer shelter; some would be sure to die,
and if out there they stumbled on a horde,

strung out, in open country, tired with marching,
the whole people could be wiped out and forgotten.
The old were against the move; Chief Mokhachane
spoke long and hoarsely, passion shooting
white jets of spittle out between his teeth.
Of all the old — as always they spoke most —
only Moshoeshoe's granddad, Peete,
spoke up for him in a trembling treble;
but when at last the vote was taken
all the young men and many middle aged
acclaimed Moshoeshoe's way. From that day he was chief.

✿

Before the stars have faded from the sky
the men have gathered, armed and ready.
Moshoeshoe and his father greet them. Leaning
on the boulder-breastworks that have served so well,
they scan the dark horizons. Nothing moves.
Under drifting bars of yellow cloud
Moshoeshoe calls men round him. At his nod,
picked runners hurry down, in twos and threes,
to take up vantage points on the nearer ridges.
Meanwhile, the clan assembles. Teenage boys
steer the few rawbone cattle up with shouts and blows.
Shivering, slow with hunger, girls and women
drag pots and baskets from the huts. Each grain
is precious, every pot, blade, strip of hide.
When a basket slips the women shriek; some run
to brush the spilling grains up in their hands.
Though armed in their best, their crescent shields adorned
with plumes like flowerspikes, their ankles, throats

and biceps ringed with brass, their foreheads decked
with ostrich feather pompoms and their spears
all honed and glinting in the yellow light,
the men are tense. They hunch in their karosses.
A cold wind flaps the feathers on their shields.
If only they could move! At last
the scouts on the ridges wave and shout — all's clear —
Moshoeshoe lifts the shield of the chief, a moon
of polished bronze you'd see five miles away.
Slowly the clan tips down the sloping path,
two thousand souls with all their goods and cattle,
warriors in front in case their force is needed;
the cattle close behind — the whole clan's life
depends on them and on the stores they carry —
the women led by 'MaMohato, boys and girls
too young for burdens, who'll catch lizards,
beetles, ants and worms, who'll grub for bulbs;
and last the dignitaries too old to fight, among them
old Peete, the only man of his generation.

In that land of lost horizons who could know
where they might blunder against enemies?
The scouts must move ahead, afraid
of being caught alone as they crossed a ridge;
but fold after desolate fold they saw
no living soul, just ruined fields, the patches
of naked earth where huts were burned, brown shards
of shattered pots, and the white bones shining
where men had died or where wild animals dragged them.

All round them was the emptiness
of once familiar places, as if man
were vanishing from earth. On easy slopes
where they'd known trim cattle kraals, fields and the woven huts
where wives ground corn at daybreak, labouring in a sound
of thocking, scraping stone, grunting, cascades of laughter;
where a man's hands knew the udders of his cows
like the grip of his shield, like the haft of his favourite axe,
as a singer knows the songs he sings or an old man knows his stories;
where after death the spirit of a man
was loved and honoured by his kin,
only the wild animals remained:
wherever earth was bare there were criss-cross tracks
of lions and leopards, jackals and hyenas,
baboons' long narrow footprints, marks of the dancing toes
of oribi and duiker, smeary tracks
of boomslang and puff adder. Once
a vulture tugged at something on a slope
of budding protea shrubs, and the wind
carried a carrion-stink they knew was human.
The men would have hurried by but Moshoeshoe stopped them.
People might still be near; in case of danger
they must wait for the weak and all move on together.

At last as darkness fell
they stopped on a little hill.
All felt the cold night swarming,
all heard the unburied dead
whose bones they'd picked their paths around
crying over crevices
bitter as the wind.
You'd think they'd have trouble sleeping,

but worn out with their marching
most fell asleep as they dropped.
Only the warrior-guards,
clutching spears and axes, faced
the terrors of the night.
Moshoeshoe walked among them.
He said, "Our dead forefathers
are standing here at our side.
Laid to rest as they should be,
honoured in the earth
with gifts of meat and beer,
even in our most hungry days,
they're stronger than the ghosts of those
that perished weak, exhausted,
in famine and despair.
No friends or children buried them,
no-one feeds them now.
All we need to fear
are living men and beasts of prey."
Then stood with them on guard.

Night thinned. Before the light the women stirred.
Still worn out from the day before
they crawled like ghosts on the smoky dawn-grey hill.
They coughed over dying fires. They blew up sparks.
They stood with pots at the stream or dragged loose stones
to grind the corn for porridge. One and all
they envied 'MaMohato; as the Chief's First Wife
she lay a little longer, warmly wrapped
in his second best kaross. None knew how her heart was chilled
at sight of the fighting men, the clan's protectors;
six months ago they were still strong;

hard knots of meat-fed muscle rode
on the long bones of their bodies. Now they lay
like fallen branches, trembling under skins,
or wandered with a dreamy slowness. Only her man
could give them fighting courage, but she knew
how cold and tense he'd come to her sleeping mat,
leaving his younger wives, to find in her arms
the warmth of understanding shared, the strength
that she alone, seeing his need, could give.

❂

Near noon, and a milder day, but the clan,
now weaker by the mile, was barely moving.
The land was wilder and more stony, paths
were broken gametracks winding between hills.
Mohale, walking by his brother, watched
the two advance scouts labour up a ridge.
Even at this slow pace, he said,
in a few hours' time they'd reach the pass.
Moshoeshoe brooded on what lay ahead.
Before they saw the next day's climb
his people needed time to forage,
resting time and a good night's sleep.

The older warriors sit, some smoking,
where light will linger longest. Wives
light fires and a team of girls
with young men to protect them go for water.

The animals are grazing. Boys
patrol them, constantly alert,
and keep them close together. One
sits on a boulder with his flute:
breathing in its quill he makes
the music feeding cattle like.

Two girls with digging sticks break up
a termites' nest — sweat flies
from their stringy arms, they look like two
demented skeletons that leap for joy
with shining eyes when they find the queen.

With cautious hands a troop of boys
go tipping rocks up to discover
worms and beetles for the pot.
They jump back whooping — they've disturbed
a rinkals. As it rears to spit,
hooded, swaying its banded throat,
they smash it down in a hail of stones.

Next morning they must face the pass.

When he saw its foot even Moshoeshoe quailed.
Through all the miles they'd trudged already,
through the horror of dead villages, the fear,
the hunger, thirst and bitter cold, at least
the hills themselves were gentle. Here
they must climb through savage country where no hut
had ever been, where thorntrees clung

to slopes of jagged rock, a breeding ground
for snakes and leopards, where the only track
was the trail of the Yellow Hunters, rutted by rains,
broken by boulders, over-hanging thorns,
and sudden hidden chasms. How could he hope
his children and his old would all get through?

Two days of climbing, agony
for Peete, struggling grimly to keep up.
Frail as a white-ant-eaten stick, he tottered
between his grandson's youngest wives, good girls
who, tired and frightened as they were, weighed down
by bundles on their heads and shoulders, scared
of predators who dog a horde, dismayed
at slipping each yard further to the rear,
kept step with the old man, murmuring words of comfort,
and held his jerking elbows.

                      Far above them,
vultures, riding on the chilly air,
picked out in him a dying animal, now seen,
now hidden under thorns, now inching on.
                              At last,
just as he knew he could struggle on no more,
slick with sweat in the cold air,
armpits raw with rubbing, every bone,
every nerve, every muscle in his body aching,
half carried by the girls, he staggered out
onto the open ridge. He'd screwed his eyes
against the sweat but the girls looked up —
before them in a flood of joy
they saw the level shining grass,

so easy underfoot, and the shining sky.
The sun was sinking westward at their backs.
The jagged walls of the Maloti loomed
ice-white ahead with gleamings like pale brass.

Somewhere right of them the path went down.

All but the stragglers were already gone.

Two women threaded between boulders glowing
with fiery lichen blooms; a little group
sat resting on the far side of the ridge.
A baby cried. A toddler tried to stand.
A pregnant woman stretched, pressing both hands
on the small of her back. None of them saw
how the cannibals of Rakotsoane
crouched in the rocks in wait. The tired girls
had time to guess the path went down near the group,
to lower Peete shaking to the ground,
to ease their loads, to stretch and sigh, no more,
before those men attacked. Light flashed
on eyes, teeth, axes; they shouted, slapped
the women, harried them, losing just one
who ducked away between rocks as the rest
were herded in a daze. Some men
had struggling babies in their arms. Moshoeshoe's wives
clung to his granddad, torn from their hands, and screamed
like wild birds as they themselves were taken.

Moshoeshoe's vanguard, striding down ahead,
caught screeches from a mile or more behind them —
instantly they doubled back, running —

up the steep slope, jumping over boulders
tearing through thorns on the narrow path.
How could the gaps have opened out so far?
Moshoeshoe's bronze shield flashed in front; the younger,
nimbler men ran just behind him. Hampered
by javelin-quivers, shields and cowhide cloaks
they dodged a confusion of goats and cattle, swinging
horns and slipping hooves, the panicky white eyes
that backed away or plunged among the herdboys.
Then it was shrieking women, 'MaMohato
shouting for calm in vain. Bewildered children
clung to their mothers. Mokhachane
hovered behind at a loss. Pausing, Moshoeshoe
ordered Mohale with the slower men
to get a grip on the women. Further up
they saw the most feeble stragglers, scattered
in helpless knots of terror, some
still struggling down the hill while others sat
rocking their heads in despair. On the crest of the ridge
a frenzied woman shrieked at the empty air.
No sign of Peete or strange warriors. No good
scrambling at random through the crags and bushes.
Hands shaking, sick at heart, Moshoeshoe knew
his frightened people must press on at once.
He alone could lead them but he sent
a score of men he chose for their hunting skills
to track the captives and attempt a rescue.

Eastward from the heights of Khamolane
gold grasses, fading to old ivory,
lean in the slanting light. There's a winding river,
now a mere winter trickle, where three eland
have drunk their fill. They move off, stepping slowly.
There's a hill in a perfect cone, and beyond,
Mohale's mountain, flat at the top, steep-sided,
crowned by a ring of cliffs. High purple hills
border the whole wide valley. On its floor,
dark drifting dots are distant troops of cattle.
You just make out the scattered kraals
where huts the colour of wild honey
are folded in low palisades. No horde
has crossed the mountains yet to drive them to the heights.

While you stand and gaze, Moshoeshoe's fittest men
are limping up — at first sight of their goal
they freeze, fling out their arms with excited cries,
take jubilant dance steps and at once
would stream downhill in disorder, leaving behind
their families and herds, but even here
Moshoeshoe knows they could be attacked.
Remember yesterday, he cries.
No stringing out; the whole of the clan must gather.
He'll lead an ordered vanguard of young men;
Mohale will bring on the rest together.

The van moves briskly, trotting downhill
to cross the river, their unspoken fear
that even since Mohale's visit someone
has occupied that mountain. As they pass

women in distant fields stand silent, watching.
A group of cowherds shout a greeting.
One sets off at a run. Moshoeshoe pauses
to hail the others; he calls that he comes in peace
and hopes for their chief's good will. Jogging on,
the Mokoteli cast enormous shadows
that waver on the grass. And now
as they draw near, the mountain seems to grow.
The crags of the summit glow like molten brass…

The approach this side is a dike that splits the cliffs.
As they labour up it over broken stone
under walls of living rock, they all feel awe:
no one could storm this place against defenders.

Moshoeshoe thinks as he climbs, forcing his mind
from Peete and the women to make plans…
The next few weeks will be hard but he smiles to see
how even now some of the men start racing.

       He's not to know
       two miles behind,
       a runner — naked for speed —
       retches his news up at Mohale's chest:
       Peete's dead and eaten.
       The women are alive.

When they reach the summit bare to the mountain winds
the twilight's falling fast and the first great stars
are shining in the east. The clan on the valley floor
are shadows lost in darkness. They scramble on the cliff

25

shouting, chattering, till their chief appears.
Then all fall silent. At his nod
a single man sends a long call below.

Before Mohale's answer comes they hear
wind-whispers over grass and stones,
a nightjar's lilting cry   the purl
of hidden springs   the sounds
they'll feel as music of their mountain mother.

As they watch Moshoeshoe still against the sky
he grows in stature as the mountain grew.

On this high grazing among stars they know
he's found his people's home. Others will come
fleeing the ruins of their shattered chiefdoms
to find protection under his wise law.

❂

My hero is Lesotho's King Moshoeshoe.
In the desolate years when wandering hordes,
driven by war and famine, ever fleeing,
spread devastation through the Sotho valleys,
when villages were burnt and stripped of cattle,
when fields were left unsown, when tribesmen hid
in caves if they could, where, sick and weak with hunger,
they ate their dogs, their clothes, their blankets, shields and sandals,
were eaten by wild beasts and ate each other,
he gathered starving refugees
and made them a new people.

Shaka

Huge and terrible and black, more dangerous than night,
than flash floods or puff adders or the raging elephant,
the king could do no wrong: at his word, or careless nod,
they hammered stakes up anuses, shattered skulls, brought night
that darkened in the dying brain forever.

Consumed by a single violent will, the spearmen of his impis
were the living flash of his power, fierce as forest fire.
They gave him rivers of enemy blood and hillsides black with corpses.

The tribe without a king was nothing, cannibals
devouring men like demons, or the lonely ghosts
who crept between dead kraals on the far side of the mountains;
lands without law, without fields, without cows, without hoes,
hyenas cracking bones in villages
where men lived once; the stick figures by the sea
who hunted crabs in pools, who scuttled behind bushes
when troops of a living people passed their way.

The Cannibals

Loathsome in skirts of human skin, they slunk self-consciously
through the hostile ranks of Mokoteli.
As they knelt at Moshoeshoe's feet, under his mountain,
their breath still stank of the human flesh they'd eaten.
Reaching his hand to touch their fearful heads,
he alone, in all that silent crowd,
could feel how those creatures, demonised by hunger,
might even now be human.

NOTES

Historical Background:
The main events of this narrative took place between 1820 and 1824, during the "lifaqane", or "time of wandering hordes". Turbulence among the Nguni peoples, east of the Drakensberg mountains, culminated in the explosive expansion of the Zulus under the warrior genius Shaka. This pushed other clans over the mountains and precipitated a cycle of destruction as one clan after another was driven onto the move. In their wake they left devastation, starvation and cannibalism born of hunger.

Characters, with a basic guide to pronunciation:

Moshoeshoe	Hero of the poem. Pronounced Mosh*wesh*weh.
Peete	Grandfather of Moshoeshoe . Pronounced Pee*heh*teh.
Mokhachane	Father of Moshoeshoe, chief of the Mokoteli. Pronounced Mokha*chan*eh.
'MaMohato	Moshoeshoe's First Wife. Her name means "mother of Mohato". Pronounced Mmamo*hah*to.
Mohale	Brother of Moshoeshoe. Pronounced Mo*hah*leh.
Mopeli	Brother of Moshoeshoe. Pronounced Mo*peh*di.
Mohlomi	Chief, diviner and healer who taught Moshoeshoe the ways of peace and justice. Pronounced Moh*lo*mi.
Rakotsoane	Leader of a cannibal band. Pronounced Rakots*wahn*eh.
'MaNtatisi	Warrior queen of the Batlokoa, the "Wild Cat People". Pronounced Mma-nta*tee*see.
Qhobosheane	Moshoeshoe's first kraal. Pronounced Qhoboshe*ah*ne

Other words:

amaHlubi	An Nguni tribe. Pronounce *Hl* like Welsh *ll*. Stress on *u*.
Kraal	An African village
Kaross	A cloak of softened skins, also used as a blanket
Nguni	A subdivision of the Bantu peoples of Southern Africa, living to the east of the Drakensberg mountains.
Oribi, duiker	Types of small antelope
Rinkals	A large venomous spitting-cobra
Sotho	Pronounced *Sutu*
Yellow Hunters	The San Bushmen